Chipmunks Do What Chipmunks Do

by Julie Verne
illustrated by Laurel Aiello

HOUGHTON MIFFLIN HARCOURT
School Publishers

Printed in China

ISBN-10: 0-547-25278-1
ISBN-13: 978-0-547-25278-0

5 6 7 8 0940 18 17 16 15 14 13 12 11 10

It is fall.

Chip looks up and sees
the birds.

They are flying south.

They look for warm weather
in the fall.

Look!
The birds are above
the tops of the trees.
Good-bye, birds!

Chip is a chipmunk.
He has to get ready
for winter, too.
So he runs into the woods.

Chip has work to do.
He gathers nuts.

Then he hides all the nuts
in his nest under
the ground.

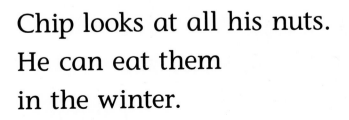

Chip looks at all his nuts.
He can eat them
in the winter.

Look!
Chip sees a raccoon
in a tree.
He sees a bear, too.
They are ready for winter.

Chipmunks sleep in the winter.
Bats sleep in the winter.
Fish sleep, too.

But Chip does not sleep
in a tree or in a pond.

He sleeps in his nest
under the ground.

Sometimes Chip wakes up
and eats his food.

Then he falls back to sleep in his warm nest.

See you in the spring!

Responding

What was the author's purpose in writing this book? Copy the chart below. Write another detail from the book that helps tell the author's purpose.

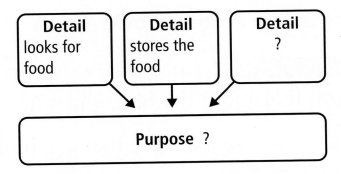

Detail	Detail	Detail
looks for food	stores the food	?

Purpose ?

Write About It

Text to Text Have you read another book about an animal in the winter? Write a paragraph. Tell what the author's purpose was in writing that story.

busy	south
chipmunks	tops
grew	turned
picked	woods

✔ **TARGET SKILL** **Author's Purpose** Tell why an author writes a book.

✔ **TARGET STRATEGY** **Analyze/Evaluate** Tell how you feel about the text, and why.

GENRE A **fantasy** is a story that could not happen in real life.